"Life Sucks! Suck It Up and Move Forward"

INTRODUCTION:

- Acknowledge the challenges and difficulties in life.

Life is full of challenges and difficulties that can sometimes feel overwhelming. It is important to acknowledge and accept these realities rather than denying or avoiding them. By recognizing the hurdles we face, we can begin to develop strategies to overcome them and move forward.

Challenges can come in various forms, such as financial struggles, health issues, relationship problems, or career setbacks. Each person's circumstances are unique, and the challenges they face may differ. It is essential to understand that everyone goes through tough times at some point or another.

Acknowledging the challenges allows us to shift our mindset from victimhood to empowerment. Rather than feeling helpless, we can take control of our lives and begin to find ways to overcome the obstacles in our path. It is through these challenges that we often discover our inner strength and resilience.

By accepting the difficulties we encounter, we can also seek support from others. Friends, family, or professionals can provide guidance, encouragement, and assistance along our journey. Sharing our struggles and seeking help is not a sign of weakness, but rather a demonstration of courage and a willingness to grow.

Remember, challenges and difficulties are a natural part of life. It is how we respond to them that truly matters. By acknowledging and embracing these challenges, we can develop the resilience and determination needed to navigate through them, ultimately leading to personal growth and a brighter future.

- Emphasize the importance of resilience and determination.

Resilience and determination are essential qualities that can help us overcome challenges and difficulties in life. They enable us to bounce back from setbacks, adapt to change, and persevere in the face of adversity.

Resilience is the ability to withstand and recover from setbacks, stress, or trauma. It involves developing a positive mindset, maintaining emotional well-being, and finding healthy coping mechanisms. Resilient individuals possess the capacity to learn from their experiences, adapt to new circumstances, and thrive despite difficult circumstances.

Determination, on the other hand, is the firmness of purpose and unwavering commitment to achieving our goals. It is the inner drive that keeps us focused, motivated, and willing to put in the necessary effort to overcome obstacles. With determination, we can push through challenges, stay focused on our objectives, and maintain a sense of purpose even when faced with setbacks.

Resilience and determination work hand in hand. When faced with challenges, resilient individuals draw on their determination to persevere. They view obstacles as opportunities for growth and learning, rather than insurmountable barriers. They maintain a positive outlook, seek solutions, and take action to overcome difficulties.

Both resilience and determination can be cultivated and strengthened over time. Developing resilience involves building a support network, practicing self-care, and cultivating a positive mindset. Determination can be nurtured by setting clear goals, breaking them down into manageable steps, and staying committed to the process.

Ultimately, resilience and determination empower us to take control of our lives and navigate through the ups and downs that come our way. They help us build the resilience needed to face challenges head-on, learn from setbacks, and ultimately achieve personal growth and success.

CHAPTER 1: ASSESSING YOUR CURRENT FINANCIAL SITUATION

- Understand your current financial status.

Understanding your current financial status is crucial for making informed decisions and planning for the future. Here are some steps to help you assess your financial situation:

1. Evaluate your income: Take stock of all your sources of income, including your salary, investments, rental income, or any other sources. Calculate your monthly or annual income to have a clear picture of your earning potential.

2. Track your expenses: Keep a record of your monthly expenses, including fixed expenses (such as rent or mortgage payments, utilities, and insurance) and variable expenses (such as groceries, transportation, entertainment, and discretionary spending). This will help you understand where your money is going and identify areas where you can potentially cut back.

3. Calculate your net worth: Determine your net worth by subtracting your liabilities (such as debts, loans, and outstanding bills) from your assets (such as savings, investments, property, and valuables). This will give you an overall snapshot of your financial health and help you understand your financial standing.

4. Review your debts: Take stock of any outstanding debts you have, such as credit card balances, student loans, or mortgages. Assess the interest rates, repayment terms, and monthly payments associated with each debt. This will help you prioritize your debt repayment strategy and manage your cash flow effectively.

5. Assess your savings and investments: Evaluate your savings accounts, emergency fund, and any investments you may have, such as stocks, bonds, or retirement accounts. Determine if you are saving enough for your short-term and long-term financial goals and consider adjusting your savings and investment strategy if necessary.

6. Consider your financial goals: Reflect on your short-term and long-term financial goals, such as buying a home, starting a business, retiring comfortably, or saving for your children's education. Assess how your current financial status aligns with these goals and identify any gaps or areas that need attention.

By understanding your current financial status, you will be better equipped to make informed decisions about budgeting, saving, investing, and managing debt. It will also help you identify areas where you can make improvements and set realistic financial goals for the future. Consider seeking professional financial advice if you need assistance in analyzing your financial situation or creating a comprehensive financial plan.

- Analyze your income, expenses, and debts.

1. Income:
Take a close look at all your sources of income, such as your salary, freelance work, rental income, or any other earnings. Calculate your monthly or annual income and make note of any fluctuations or irregularities. This will give you a clear understanding of your earning potential and help you plan your budget accordingly.

2. Expenses:
Track your monthly expenses to gain insight into your spending habits. Categorize your expenses into fixed and variable categories. Fixed expenses include items like rent or mortgage payments, utilities, insurance, and loan repayments, while variable expenses include groceries, transportation,

entertainment, and discretionary spending. Analyzing your expenses will help you identify areas where you can potentially cut back and save more.

3. Debts:

Assess your outstanding debts, such as credit card balances, student loans, personal loans, or mortgages. Make a list of each debt, noting the interest rates, repayment terms, and monthly payments associated with them. This will help you understand the total amount of debt you owe and the impact it has on your finances. Prioritize your debts based on interest rates and create a repayment plan to gradually reduce and eliminate them.

Analyzing your income, expenses, and debts will provide you with a comprehensive view of your financial situation. It will help you identify areas where you can make adjustments, such as increasing your income, reducing expenses, or paying off debts more aggressively. This analysis will enable you to make informed decisions about budgeting, saving, investing, and managing your financial goals effectively.

- Set realistic financial goals.

Setting realistic financial goals is crucial for your financial well-being. Here's a step-by-step process to help you set achievable financial goals:

1. Evaluate your current financial situation: Assess your income, expenses, debts, and savings. Understand where you stand financially and identify any areas for improvement.

2. Define your short-term and long-term goals: Short-term goals typically span within a year, such as building an emergency fund or paying off a credit card. Long-term goals extend beyond a year, such as saving for a down payment on a house or retirement. Clearly define your goals and prioritize them based on their importance to you.

3. Make your goals specific and measurable: Instead of setting a vague goal like "save money," specify the amount you want to save and by when. For example, "Save $5,000 for a vacation in 12 months." This makes your goal more tangible and helps you track your progress.

4. Ensure your goals are realistic: Consider your current financial situation, including your income, expenses, and existing commitments. Set goals that are challenging but attainable. Unrealistic goals can lead to frustration and disappointment, while achievable goals provide motivation and a sense of accomplishment.

5. Break down your goals into actionable steps: Divide your goals into smaller milestones or actions that you can work on incrementally. For example, if your goal is to pay off a credit card debt of $5,000, break it down into monthly payments or a specific amount to be paid off each month.

6. Set a timeline: Assign a target date to each goal. This will help you stay focused and motivated, knowing that you have a specific deadline to work towards.

7. Regularly review and adjust your goals: Financial circumstances and priorities may change over time. Review your goals periodically and make adjustments as needed. Celebrate your achievements along the way and stay committed to your financial goals.

Remember, setting realistic financial goals is about finding a balance between ambition and practicality. By following these steps, you'll be on your way to achieving financial success.

CHAPTER 2: CREATING A BUDGET

- Learn how to create a practical budget.

Creating a practical budget is essential for managing your finances effectively. Here's a step-by-step guide to help you create a budget:

1. Track your income and expenses: Start by gathering all your financial information, including income sources (salary, investments, etc.) and expenses (bills, groceries, entertainment, etc.). Track your expenses for a month to get a clear picture of where your money is going.

2. Categorize your expenses: Categorize your expenses into different categories like housing, transportation, food, entertainment, debt repayment, savings, etc. This will help you understand your spending patterns and identify areas where you can make adjustments.

3. Determine your income and savings goals: Set financial goals based on your income and priorities. Decide how much you want to save each month and allocate a portion of your income towards savings or investments.

4. Create a monthly budget: Now that you have a clear understanding of your income, expenses, and goals, create a monthly budget. Start by allocating money for essentials like housing, utilities, transportation, and groceries. Then assign amounts for discretionary expenses like entertainment and dining out. Finally, prioritize savings and debt repayment by allocating a portion of your income towards these goals.

5. Track your budget: Use a spreadsheet, budgeting app, or pen

and paper to track your income and expenses. Update it regularly to ensure you are staying within your budgeted amounts. This will help you identify any overspending and make necessary adjustments.

6. Make adjustments as needed: Periodically review your budget to see if it aligns with your financial goals and lifestyle. Adjust your budget as circumstances change or new expenses arise. Be flexible and willing to adapt to ensure your budget remains practical and effective.

7. Monitor your progress: Regularly review your budget to monitor your progress towards your financial goals. Celebrate milestones and make adjustments if you find yourself falling behind or exceeding your targets.

Remember, creating a practical budget requires discipline and consistency. It may take time to find the right balance, so be patient with yourself. By following these steps, you'll be on your way to better financial management and achieving your financial goals.

- Identify areas where you can cut expenses.

Identifying areas where you can cut expenses is an important part of creating a practical budget. Here are some common areas where you can potentially reduce your expenses:

1. Evaluate discretionary spending: Take a close look at your discretionary spending, such as dining out, entertainment, subscriptions, and impulse purchases. Consider reducing or eliminating some of these expenses to free up more money in your budget.

2. Review your utility bills: Examine your utility bills, such as electricity, water, and internet. Look for ways to reduce usage, such as turning off lights when not in use, using energy-efficient appliances, or negotiating a better internet plan.

3. Cut back on groceries: Review your grocery shopping habits and see if there are areas where you can save. Consider planning meals in advance, buying store brands or generic products, using coupons, and avoiding unnecessary impulse purchases.

4. Reduce transportation costs: Evaluate your transportation expenses, including fuel, public transportation, or car maintenance. Explore options like carpooling, using public transportation more often, or downsizing to a more fuel-efficient vehicle if feasible.

5. Negotiate bills and monthly subscriptions: Contact your service providers such as internet, cable, or insurance companies, and negotiate better rates or switch to cheaper alternatives. Also, review your monthly subscriptions and cancel any that you no longer use or need.

6. Minimize eating out: Eating out frequently can add up quickly. Consider limiting dining out to special occasions and opt for cooking at home more often. Preparing meals at home not only saves money but also allows you to have more control over ingredients and portion sizes.

7. Reassess your entertainment expenses: Look for alternative, low-cost or free entertainment options like community events, parks, or libraries. Consider reducing expenses on movie tickets, concerts, or memberships to clubs or gyms if you find them to be excessive.

Remember, cutting expenses doesn't mean completely depriving yourself. It's about finding a balance and prioritizing your financial goals. By identifying areas where you can reduce expenses, you can make more room in your budget for savings, debt repayment, or other important financial priorities.

- Allocate funds towards your financial goals.

Allocating funds towards your financial goals is a crucial step in achieving them. Here's how you can do it effectively:

1. Set clear financial goals: Start by identifying your short-term and long-term financial goals. Whether it's saving for a down payment on a house, building an emergency fund, paying off debt, or planning for retirement, having specific goals will help you prioritize your financial decisions.

2. Create a budget: Develop a budget that outlines your income, expenses, and savings. Allocate a portion of your income towards each of your financial goals. This will give you a clear understanding of how much you need to set aside each month to achieve those goals.

3. Prioritize your goals: Determine which goals are most important to you and allocate funds accordingly. Some goals may require more immediate attention, while others can be addressed over a longer period. Prioritizing helps you focus your financial resources where they are needed the most.

4. Automate savings: Consider setting up automatic transfers from your checking account to separate savings accounts dedicated to each financial goal. This ensures that a portion of your income is consistently being saved towards your goals without the temptation to spend it elsewhere.

5. Reduce unnecessary expenses: Look for areas in your budget where you can cut back on expenses. By reducing discretionary spending and finding ways to save on everyday expenses, you can free up more funds to allocate towards your financial goals.

6. Increase your income: Explore opportunities to increase your income, such as taking on a side gig, freelancing, or negotiating a raise at work. Increasing your earning potential can provide you with additional funds to allocate towards your financial goals.

7. Regularly review and adjust: Periodically review your progress towards your financial goals and make adjustments as needed.

Life circumstances and priorities may change, requiring you to reallocate funds or set new goals.

Remember, consistency and discipline are key when allocating funds towards your financial goals. By making intentional choices and regularly monitoring your progress, you can make significant strides towards achieving your financial aspirations.

CHAPTER 3: BUILDING AN EMERGENCY FUND

- Understand the significance of having an emergency fund.

Having an emergency fund is crucial for financial stability and peace of mind. Here's why it's significant:

1. Financial security: An emergency fund acts as a safety net during unexpected events such as medical emergencies, job loss, or major home repairs. It provides a financial cushion that allows you to handle these situations without relying on credit cards, loans, or depleting your savings meant for other goals.

2. Unforeseen expenses: Life is full of surprises, and many of these surprises come with unexpected expenses. Whether it's a car repair, a sudden medical bill, or a home appliance breaking down, having an emergency fund ensures that you're prepared to handle these unforeseen costs without disrupting your regular budget or going into debt.

3. Peace of mind: Knowing that you have a dedicated fund for emergencies can significantly reduce financial stress and anxiety. It provides a sense of security, knowing that you have a financial buffer to rely on in times of crisis. This peace of mind allows you to focus on other aspects of your life without constant worry about unexpected financial burdens.

4. Avoiding debt: Without an emergency fund, many people resort to borrowing money or using credit cards to cover unexpected expenses. This can lead to high-interest debt and a cycle of financial strain. Having an emergency fund allows you to avoid taking on unnecessary debt and the associated interest payments.

5. Flexibility and opportunity: An emergency fund not only protects you from unexpected expenses but also provides you with the flexibility to pursue opportunities. It can be used as a starting point for a new business venture, to invest in education or professional development, or to take advantage of a time-limited opportunity. Having a financial safety net gives you the freedom to make choices that align with your long-term goals.

6. Financial resilience: Building an emergency fund is an essential step in developing financial resilience. It helps you bounce back from unexpected setbacks, maintain financial independence, and continue working towards your other financial goals, such as saving for retirement or buying a home.

In summary, an emergency fund is a fundamental component of a strong financial foundation. It provides financial security, peace of mind, and the ability to handle unexpected expenses, while also allowing you to maintain your financial independence and pursue opportunities. It's a proactive step towards building a stable and resilient financial future.

- Discover strategies to save money for unexpected expenses.

Saving money for unexpected expenses requires discipline and a thoughtful approach. Here are some strategies to help you save effectively:

1. Set a budget: Create a budget that includes your income, expenses, and savings goals. Be realistic about your spending habits and identify areas where you can cut back. Allocate a portion of your income specifically for saving towards unexpected expenses.

2. Automate savings: Set up automatic transfers from your checking account to a separate savings account dedicated to emergency funds. This can help you save consistently without the temptation to spend the money elsewhere.

3. Start small, increase gradually: If saving seems overwhelming, start with small contributions and gradually increase them over time. Even saving a small amount regularly can add up over time and provide a safety net for unexpected expenses.

4. Track and reduce expenses: Monitor your spending habits and identify areas where you can cut back. Consider reducing discretionary expenses like eating out, entertainment, or unnecessary subscriptions. Redirect the money saved towards your emergency fund.

5. Save windfalls and bonuses: Use unexpected windfalls such as tax refunds, bonuses, or any unexpected sources of income to boost your emergency fund. Instead of splurging, consider putting a portion or the entire amount into your savings.

6. Cut unnecessary subscriptions: Review your subscriptions and memberships regularly. Cancel any services you no longer use or find alternatives that offer similar benefits at a lower cost. Redirect the money saved towards your emergency fund.

7. Create an "emergency fund jar": Keep a jar or container in your home where you can deposit loose change or small bills regularly. This can be an additional way to save money gradually without feeling the impact on your daily budget.

8. Reduce debt: High-interest debt can drain your resources and make it challenging to save for unexpected expenses. Prioritize paying off debt to free up more funds for saving. Consider using the snowball or avalanche method to pay off debts systematically.

9. Shop smart and comparison shop: Before making a purchase, compare prices from different stores or online platforms. Look for discounts, coupons, or sales to save money on your regular purchases. The money saved can be directed towards your emergency fund.

10. Stay motivated: Set clear goals for yourself and remind

yourself of the importance of having an emergency fund. Celebrate milestones along the way to keep yourself motivated. Consider visualizing the peace of mind and financial security that comes with having a well-funded emergency fund.

Remember, saving for unexpected expenses is a long-term commitment. By implementing these strategies, you can gradually build a robust emergency fund that will provide financial security and help you navigate unexpected situations without unnecessary stress.

- Set a specific target for your emergency fund.

Setting a specific target for your emergency fund will depend on your individual circumstances and financial goals. As a general guideline, it is recommended to aim for saving three to six months' worth of living expenses. This amount can provide a buffer to cover unexpected expenses, such as medical bills, car repairs, or job loss.

To determine the exact target for your emergency fund, consider the following factors:

1. Monthly expenses: Calculate your average monthly expenses, including rent/mortgage, utilities, groceries, transportation, debt payments, insurance, and any other essential costs.

2. Job stability: Assess the stability of your income. If you have a stable job or multiple sources of income, saving three months' worth of expenses might be sufficient. However, if your income is unpredictable or you work on a contractual basis, aiming for six months' worth of expenses may offer more security.

3. Dependents and personal circumstances: Consider your personal situation. If you have dependents or specific financial obligations, such as supporting a family or mortgage payments, you may want to save a higher amount to account for those factors.

4. Risk tolerance: Evaluate your comfort level with risk. If you have a higher risk tolerance or access to other forms of financial support, you may opt for a smaller emergency fund. Conversely, if you prefer a greater safety net, you might aim for a larger emergency fund.

Remember, setting a specific target for your emergency fund is a starting point. As your financial situation evolves, you can reassess and adjust the target accordingly. Regularly review your emergency fund and make necessary adjustments based on changes in your income, expenses, and financial goals.

CHAPTER 4: MANAGING DEBT

- Implement effective strategies to manage and reduce debt.

Managing and reducing debt requires a combination of disciplined financial habits and effective strategies. Here are some steps you can take:

1. Create a budget: Start by tracking your income and expenses to get a clear picture of your financial situation. Create a budget that prioritizes debt repayment and allows for necessary expenses. Cut back on non-essential expenses to free up more money for debt payments.

2. Prioritize debt payments: Make a list of your debts, including the interest rates and minimum payments for each. Prioritize your debts by focusing on paying off high-interest debt first, while making minimum payments on other debts. This strategy can save you money on interest payments in the long run.

3. Negotiate interest rates: Contact your creditors and explore the possibility of negotiating lower interest rates. This can help reduce the overall cost of your debt and make it easier to pay off.

4. Snowball or avalanche method: Consider using either the snowball or avalanche method to pay off your debts. With the snowball method, you pay off the smallest debt first and then move on to the next one, creating a sense of accomplishment. With the avalanche method, you prioritize debts with the highest interest rates first to save on interest costs.

5. Consolidate or refinance: Explore the option of consolidating your debts into a single loan with a lower interest rate. This can simplify your payments and potentially save you money.

Similarly, if you have high-interest loans, consider refinancing them to secure a lower interest rate.

6. Increase your income: Look for ways to increase your income, such as taking on a part-time job or freelancing. The additional income can be used to accelerate debt repayment.

7. Seek professional help if needed: If you're overwhelmed by your debt, consider consulting a credit counselor or financial advisor. They can provide guidance and help you create a personalized plan to manage and reduce your debt.

Remember, managing and reducing debt takes time and discipline. Stay committed to your plan, avoid taking on new debt, and celebrate small victories along the way.

- Explore techniques such as debt consolidation or negotiation.

Debt consolidation and negotiation are two effective techniques for managing and reducing debt. Here's a closer look at each approach:

1. Debt consolidation: Debt consolidation involves combining multiple debts into a single loan or credit card with a lower interest rate. This can simplify your payments and potentially save you money on interest payments. Here's how you can consolidate your debt:

a. Balance transfer credit card: Transfer your high-interest credit card balances to a new credit card with a lower or 0% introductory interest rate. Make sure to read the terms and conditions, including any balance transfer fees or the duration of the promotional interest rate.

b. Personal loan: Apply for a personal loan with a lower interest rate than your current debts. Use the loan proceeds to pay off your high-interest debts. This strategy can help streamline your payments and potentially save on interest costs.

c. Home equity loan or line of credit: If you own a home, you may be able to use your home's equity to secure a loan or line of credit with a lower interest rate. However, this option requires careful consideration as your home is used as collateral.

2. Debt negotiation: Debt negotiation involves reaching out to your creditors to negotiate a lower interest rate, a reduced payoff amount, or a more manageable repayment plan. Here's how to approach debt negotiation:

a. Communicate with your creditors: Contact your creditors and explain your financial situation honestly. Discuss your willingness to pay but highlight the challenges you are facing. Ask if they are open to negotiating new terms that are more favorable to you.

b. Seek professional help: If negotiating with creditors feels overwhelming, consider working with a reputable credit counseling agency. They can negotiate on your behalf and help you create a debt management plan.

c. Get everything in writing: If you reach an agreement with your creditors, make sure to get the new terms in writing. This ensures that both parties are clear on the agreed-upon changes.

Remember, both debt consolidation and negotiation are strategies that require careful consideration and planning. Evaluate your options, compare interest rates, and consider seeking professional advice if needed to make informed decisions that align with your financial goals.

- Develop a plan to pay off your debts systematically.

Developing a systematic plan to pay off your debts can help you stay organized and motivated. Here's a step-by-step approach to creating a debt repayment plan:

1. Assess your debts: Start by gathering all the necessary

information about your debts, including the outstanding balances, interest rates, minimum monthly payments, and due dates. This will give you a clear picture of your overall debt situation.

2. Prioritize your debts: Determine which debts to focus on first. You have two common methods to consider:

a. Avalanche method: Arrange your debts in order of their interest rates, starting from the highest. Allocate extra payments towards the debt with the highest interest rate while making minimum payments on the other debts. Once the highest-interest debt is paid off, move on to the next one.

b. Snowball method: Arrange your debts in order of their outstanding balances, starting from the smallest. Allocate extra payments towards the debt with the smallest balance while making minimum payments on the other debts. Once the smallest debt is paid off, move on to the next one.

3. Set a budget: Review your income and expenses to create a realistic budget. Allocate a portion of your income towards debt repayment while ensuring you have enough for essential expenses. Cut back on non-essential spending to free up more funds for debt repayment.

4. Increase your income: Consider ways to boost your income, such as taking on a part-time job, freelancing, or selling unused items. The additional income can be dedicated towards paying off your debts more quickly.

5. Negotiate lower interest rates: Contact your creditors and inquire about the possibility of reducing your interest rates. Lower interest rates can help you save money and pay off your debts faster. Be prepared to explain your financial situation and provide reasons why you deserve a lower rate.

6. Track your progress: Keep a record of your payments and

monitor your progress regularly. Celebrate milestones along the way to stay motivated. There are various budgeting apps and spreadsheets available that can help you track your debt repayment journey.

7. Stay committed: It's essential to remain committed to your debt repayment plan. Stick to your budget, avoid taking on new debt, and resist the temptation to overspend. Remember that the sacrifices you make now will lead to financial freedom in the future.

By following these steps and staying dedicated to your plan, you can systematically pay off your debts, regain control of your finances, and achieve your financial goals.

CHAPTER 5: INCREASING INCOME OPPORTUNITIES

- Explore different ways to increase your income.

1. Take on a side gig or freelance work: Consider leveraging your skills and interests by taking on part-time or freelance work. This can include freelance writing, graphic design, tutoring, pet sitting, or driving for ride-sharing services. Online platforms like Upwork, Fiverr, and TaskRabbit can help you find gigs.

2. Start a small business: If you have an entrepreneurial spirit, starting a small business can be a great way to generate additional income. Identify a product or service that you can offer, and create a business plan to guide your efforts. This could be anything from selling handmade crafts online to offering consulting services in your area of expertise.

3. Rent out a spare room or property: If you have an extra room or property, consider renting it out through platforms like Airbnb or VRBO. This can be a lucrative way to earn extra income, especially if you live in a popular tourist destination or near a major event venue.

4. Monetize your hobbies or talents: Do you have a hobby or talent that you could turn into a source of income? For example, if you enjoy photography, you could offer photography services for events or sell your prints online. If you're skilled in a particular instrument, you could give music lessons.

5. Explore online opportunities: The internet offers numerous opportunities to earn income. You can start a blog or a YouTube channel and monetize it through advertising or sponsored

content. Additionally, you can participate in online surveys, become an affiliate marketer, or sell products through an online store.

6. Rent out your belongings: If you have valuable items that you don't use often, consider renting them out. This could include camera equipment, power tools, camping gear, or even your car. Platforms like Fat Llama and Turo allow you to rent out your belongings to others for a fee.

7. Take advantage of your skills and expertise: Assess your professional skills and expertise. You could offer consulting services or become a freelancer in your industry. Many companies and individuals are willing to pay for specialized knowledge and experience.

Remember, exploring different income-boosting opportunities requires effort, dedication, and sometimes investment. It's important to consider your own interests, skills, and available time when choosing the right income-boosting option for you.

- Consider options like freelancing, part-time work, or side businesses.

Let's dive deeper into these options:

1. Freelancing: Freelancing allows you to work on projects or assignments for various clients on a contract basis. You can offer services such as writing, graphic design, web development, social media management, or virtual assistance. Platforms like Upwork, Freelancer, and Fiverr connect freelancers with clients looking for specific skills.

2. Part-time work: Taking on a part-time job can be a great way to supplement your income. Look for opportunities in industries such as retail, hospitality, customer service, or delivery services. You can also explore remote part-time job options that offer flexibility and the ability to work from home.

3. Side businesses: Starting a side business can be a rewarding way to increase your income. Identify a product or service that you are passionate about, and develop a business plan. This could be anything from starting an online store, offering consulting services, or even creating and selling your own products. Launching a side business requires careful planning, market research, and dedication.

4. Online platforms and marketplaces: There are numerous online platforms and marketplaces where you can sell products or offer services. Consider platforms like Etsy for handmade goods, Amazon for product sales, or Udemy for online courses. These platforms provide a ready-made audience and can help you reach customers around the world.

5. Renting or sharing assets: If you have assets that are underutilized, you can consider sharing or renting them out. For example, you can rent out a spare room, parking space, or even equipment like cameras, power tools, or camping gear. Platforms like Airbnb, Turo, and Fat Llama facilitate these types of transactions.

6. Monetizing your hobbies: If you have a hobby or passion, explore ways to monetize it. For instance, if you enjoy photography, you can offer photography services for events or sell your prints online. If you're skilled in crafts, you can create and sell your handmade products. Look for opportunities to turn your hobbies into income-generating ventures.

Remember, when exploring these options, it's important to consider your skills, interests, and available time. Choose an option that aligns with your strengths and provides a sense of fulfillment. It may take some time and effort to establish yourself, but with dedication, these options can help increase your income.

- Develop skills and pursue opportunities for career growth.

Developing your skills and pursuing opportunities for career growth is essential for increasing your income. Here are some steps you can take:

1. Identify your goals: Start by determining your long-term career goals and the skills you need to achieve them. This will help you focus your efforts on the areas that will have the most impact.

2. Assess your current skills: Take stock of your existing skills and knowledge. Identify any gaps between your current skill set and what is required for your desired career path. This will help you prioritize which skills to develop.

3. Continuous learning: Commit to lifelong learning and skill development. Take advantage of online courses, workshops, webinars, and industry certifications. Platforms like Coursera, LinkedIn Learning, and Udemy offer a wide range of courses to enhance your skills.

4. Networking: Build a strong professional network by attending industry events, joining relevant online communities, and connecting with professionals in your field. Networking can open doors to new opportunities, mentorship, and valuable insights.

5. Seek challenges and new responsibilities: Look for opportunities to take on additional responsibilities or challenging projects within your current job. This can help you develop new skills and demonstrate your potential for growth.

6. Volunteer or intern: Consider volunteering or interning in your desired field to gain practical experience and expand your network. This can also help you demonstrate your skills and commitment to prospective employers.

7. Stay updated with industry trends: Keep yourself informed about the latest trends, technologies, and advancements in your industry. This will help you stay ahead of the curve and remain competitive.

8. Set clear career goals: Define short-term and long-term career goals. Break them down into actionable steps and create a timeline to track your progress. Regularly reassess your goals and make adjustments as needed.

Remember, career growth and skill development take time and effort. Be proactive, stay motivated, and embrace opportunities that come your way. With dedication and a growth mindset, you can increase your income and achieve your career aspirations.

CHAPTER 6: INVESTING FOR THE FUTURE

- Understand the basics of investing.

1. Define your financial goals: Clearly identify what you want to achieve through investing. Whether it's saving for retirement, buying a house, or funding your children's education, having specific goals will guide your investment decisions.

2. Educate yourself: Take the time to learn about different investment options, such as stocks, bonds, mutual funds, and real estate. Understand the risks, potential returns, and how each investment aligns with your goals.

3. Assess your risk tolerance: Evaluate your comfort level with taking risks. Investments with higher potential returns often come with greater volatility and the potential for losses. Determine your risk tolerance to help you choose the right investment strategy.

4. Diversify your portfolio: Don't put all your eggs in one basket. Diversification involves spreading your investments across different asset classes, sectors, and geographical regions. This helps mitigate risk and allows your portfolio to benefit from multiple sources of growth.

5. Start investing early: Time is your ally when it comes to investing. The power of compounding allows your investments to grow exponentially over time. The earlier you start, the more time your investments have to grow and recover from any short-term market fluctuations.

6. Create an investment plan: Develop a well-thought-out investment plan that aligns with your goals, risk tolerance, and

time horizon. Consider consulting with a financial advisor who can provide personalized guidance based on your specific needs.

7. Regularly review and adjust: Monitor your investments regularly and make adjustments as needed. Market conditions, economic factors, and personal circumstances may warrant modifications to your investment strategy.

8. Stay informed: Stay updated on financial news, market trends, and economic indicators. This will help you make informed decisions and adapt your investment approach accordingly.

9. Patience and long-term perspective: Investing is a long-term game. Avoid making impulsive decisions based on short-term market fluctuations. Stick to your investment plan and have faith in the power of compounding over time.

Remember, investing involves risks, and past performance is not indicative of future results. It's advisable to consult with a financial professional who can provide personalized advice based on your unique situation.

- Learn about different investment options such as stocks, bonds, or real estate.

1. Stocks: Buying shares of stock means becoming a partial owner of a company. Stocks offer potential for capital appreciation (increase in share price) and dividends (portion of company profits distributed to shareholders). However, stocks can be volatile, and their value can fluctuate based on market conditions and company performance.

2. Bonds: Bonds are debt instruments issued by governments, municipalities, or corporations to raise capital. When you buy a bond, you are essentially lending money to the issuer in exchange for periodic interest payments and return of the principal amount at maturity. Bonds are generally considered lower-risk investments than stocks, but they offer lower potential returns.

3. Mutual Funds: Mutual funds pool money from multiple investors to invest in a diversified portfolio of stocks, bonds, or other assets. They are managed by professional fund managers. Mutual funds offer diversification, as well as the convenience of professional management. They are available in different types, such as equity funds, bond funds, or balanced funds, catering to various investment objectives.

4. Exchange-Traded Funds (ETFs): ETFs are similar to mutual funds but trade on stock exchanges like individual stocks. They offer diversification and can track various market indexes or specific sectors. ETFs can be bought and sold throughout the trading day, and their prices can fluctuate based on supply and demand.

5. Real Estate: Investing in real estate involves purchasing properties with the aim of generating income and/or capital appreciation. Real estate can include residential, commercial, or industrial properties. Potential returns come from rental income and property value appreciation. Real estate investments can offer diversification, but they often require larger upfront capital, ongoing maintenance, and market knowledge.

6. Commodities: Commodities include tangible assets like gold, silver, oil, natural gas, agricultural products, and more. Investors can gain exposure to commodities through various means, such as commodity futures contracts, commodity-focused mutual funds, or ETFs. Commodities can provide a hedge against inflation and diversification, but they can also be volatile.

Remember, each investment option comes with its own risks and potential returns. It's important to consider your financial goals, risk tolerance, and time horizon when choosing the right mix of investments. Consulting with a financial advisor can help you navigate the complexities and make informed investment decisions.

- Seek professional advice to make informed investment decisions.

Seeking professional advice is always a wise step when making investment decisions. A financial advisor can provide valuable insights tailored to your specific financial goals, risk tolerance, and time horizon. They can help you understand the intricacies of different investment options, analyze your current financial situation, and develop a personalized investment strategy.

When choosing a financial advisor, consider their qualifications, experience, and reputation. Look for professionals who are registered with regulatory bodies and adhere to ethical standards. You may also want to inquire about their fee structure to ensure it aligns with your preferences.

A financial advisor can assist you in assessing your risk appetite, diversifying your portfolio, and monitoring your investments over time. They can also provide guidance during market fluctuations and help you stay focused on your long-term goals.

Remember, while a financial advisor can offer valuable advice, it's important to actively participate in the decision-making process. Ask questions, understand the investment recommendations, and make sure they align with your financial objectives.

By working with a trusted financial advisor, you can make more informed investment decisions and increase your chances of achieving your financial goals.

CHAPTER 7: PRIORITIZING PHYSICAL WELL-BEING

- Highlight the importance of physical health.

Physical health is of utmost importance for overall well-being and quality of life. It plays a crucial role in our ability to perform daily activities, pursue our passions, and enjoy life to the fullest. Here are some key reasons why physical health is important:

1. Disease Prevention: Regular exercise and a healthy lifestyle can help prevent a range of chronic diseases such as heart disease, diabetes, obesity, and certain types of cancer. Physical activity boosts the immune system, strengthens the body's defenses, and enhances overall resilience.

2. Mental Well-being: Physical health has a direct impact on mental health. Regular exercise releases endorphins, which are natural mood boosters, and reduces stress and anxiety. It can also improve sleep patterns, enhance cognitive function, and contribute to better mental clarity and focus.

3. Energy and Vitality: Engaging in regular physical activity increases energy levels and improves stamina, making daily tasks and activities more manageable. It promotes better cardiovascular health, strengthens muscles and bones, and enhances overall physical endurance.

4. Longevity and Quality of Life: Maintaining good physical health is strongly linked to a longer and healthier life. By adopting a healthy lifestyle that includes regular exercise, a balanced diet, and adequate rest, individuals can reduce the risk of premature aging and age-related diseases, and enjoy a higher quality of life as

they age.

5. Self-Confidence and Self-Esteem: Taking care of our physical health positively impacts our self-image and self-perception. Regular exercise can improve body image, boost self-confidence, and enhance self-esteem. It promotes a sense of accomplishment and empowers individuals to set and achieve personal fitness goals.

6. Improved Productivity: Physical health has a direct correlation to productivity and performance in various aspects of life. By maintaining good physical health, individuals experience increased focus, higher energy levels, and improved cognitive function, leading to enhanced productivity in work, studies, and daily activities.

Remember, physical health is a lifelong commitment. It's important to engage in regular exercise, eat a balanced diet, stay hydrated, get enough sleep, and avoid harmful habits like smoking or excessive alcohol consumption. Consulting with healthcare professionals and following their advice can also contribute to maintaining and improving physical health.

- Discuss strategies for maintaining a healthy lifestyle.

Maintaining a healthy lifestyle involves incorporating various strategies into your daily routine. Here are some key strategies to help you maintain a healthy lifestyle:

1. Regular Physical Activity: Engage in regular exercise or physical activity that you enjoy. Aim for at least 150 minutes of moderate-intensity aerobic activity or 75 minutes of vigorous-intensity activity per week. This can include activities like walking, jogging, cycling, swimming, or dancing. Additionally, include strength training exercises at least twice a week to improve muscle strength and endurance.

2. Balanced and Nutritious Diet: Focus on consuming a balanced

diet that includes a variety of fruits, vegetables, whole grains, lean proteins, and healthy fats. Limit your intake of processed foods, sugary snacks, and beverages. Practice portion control and opt for homemade meals whenever possible. Stay hydrated by drinking an adequate amount of water throughout the day.

3. Adequate Sleep: Prioritize getting enough sleep to support your overall health. Aim for 7-9 hours of quality sleep each night. Establish a consistent sleep routine, create a sleep-friendly environment, and limit the use of electronic devices before bedtime to improve sleep quality.

4. Stress Management: Implement stress management techniques to reduce the negative impact of stress on your health. This can include activities such as meditation, deep breathing exercises, yoga, journaling, or engaging in hobbies that help you relax and unwind. Prioritize self-care and make time for activities that bring you joy and relaxation.

5. Regular Health Check-ups: Schedule regular check-ups with your healthcare provider to monitor your health, identify any potential issues, and take preventive measures. This includes screenings for various conditions like blood pressure, cholesterol levels, and cancer screenings as recommended based on age and gender.

6. Limit Sedentary Behavior: Minimize prolonged periods of sitting or inactivity. Incorporate movement breaks throughout the day, whether it's taking a short walk, stretching, or doing some light exercises. Consider using a standing desk or taking the stairs instead of the elevator whenever possible.

7. Social Connections: Foster and maintain positive relationships with family, friends, and the community. Social connections contribute to overall well-being and can provide support during challenging times.

8. Avoid Harmful Habits: Minimize or eliminate harmful habits

such as smoking, excessive alcohol consumption, or drug use. These habits can have detrimental effects on your health and well-being.

Remember, creating a healthy lifestyle is a gradual process. Start by incorporating small changes into your daily routine and gradually build upon them. It's important to listen to your body, be kind to yourself, and seek professional guidance when needed.

- Provide tips on exercise, nutrition, and self-care practices.

Exercise:
1. Find an activity you enjoy: Choose exercises or physical activities that you genuinely enjoy, whether it's dancing, hiking, swimming, or playing a sport. This will make it easier to stick to a regular exercise routine.

2. Mix it up: Incorporate a variety of exercises into your routine to keep it interesting and target different muscle groups. This can include cardio exercises like running or cycling, strength training with weights or resistance bands, and flexibility exercises like yoga or Pilates.

3. Set realistic goals: Set specific, achievable goals to keep yourself motivated. Whether it's increasing the number of steps you take in a day or working towards completing a specific fitness milestone, having goals can help you stay focused and track your progress.

Nutrition:
1. Eat a balanced diet: Focus on consuming a variety of whole foods, including fruits, vegetables, whole grains, lean proteins, and healthy fats. Aim for a balanced plate that includes all major food groups.

2. Portion control: Pay attention to portion sizes to avoid overeating. Use smaller plates and bowls, and listen to your body's hunger and fullness cues to avoid mindless eating.

3. Meal planning and preparation: Plan and prepare your meals in advance to make healthier choices easier. This can help you avoid relying on unhealthy convenience foods when you're short on time or feeling hungry.

Self-Care:
1. Prioritize sleep: Make sleep a priority and ensure you're getting enough restful sleep each night. Establish a regular sleep routine and create a relaxing environment in your bedroom.

2. Practice stress management: Find healthy ways to manage stress, such as practicing mindfulness or meditation, engaging in hobbies, or spending time in nature. Take breaks when needed and give yourself permission to rest and recharge.

3. Engage in activities you enjoy: Make time for activities that bring you joy and relaxation, whether it's reading, listening to music, taking a bath, or spending time with loved ones. Self-care is essential for overall well-being.

4. Practice self-compassion: Be kind to yourself and practice self-compassion. Treat yourself with the same kindness and understanding you would show to a friend. Celebrate your successes, no matter how small, and don't be too hard on yourself when faced with setbacks.

Remember, everyone's needs and preferences are different, so it's important to find what works best for you. Start by incorporating small changes into your routine and gradually build upon them. Listen to your body, seek professional guidance when needed, and be patient with yourself as you navigate your health and well-being journey.

CHAPTER 8: OVERCOMING SETBACKS AND STAYING MOTIVATED

- Address the inevitable setbacks and challenges in life.

Setbacks and challenges are a natural part of life. Here are some suggestions on how to address them:

1. Acceptance and resilience: Accept that setbacks and challenges are a normal part of life. Instead of dwelling on what went wrong, focus on building resilience and finding ways to bounce back. Remember that setbacks do not define you; it's how you respond to them that matters.

2. Positive mindset: Cultivate a positive mindset by reframing setbacks as opportunities for growth and learning. Embrace the idea that challenges can lead to personal development and new possibilities. Practice gratitude and focus on what is going well in your life, even during difficult times.

3. Seek support: Reach out to friends, family, or a support network when facing setbacks. Sharing your thoughts and feelings with others can provide emotional support and fresh perspectives. Don't hesitate to seek professional help if needed, such as speaking with a therapist or counselor.

4. Break it down: When faced with a major challenge, break it down into smaller, more manageable steps. This can make the situation seem less overwhelming and help you create an action plan to move forward.

5. Learn from setbacks: Take the opportunity to learn from setbacks and mistakes. Reflect on what went wrong, identify any patterns, and consider what you can do differently next time. Use

setbacks as valuable lessons to grow and improve.

6. Self-care and self-compassion: During challenging times, prioritize self-care and self-compassion. Take care of your physical and emotional well-being by engaging in activities that bring you joy and relaxation. Treat yourself with kindness and understanding, practicing self-compassion rather than self-criticism.

7. Stay flexible and adaptable: Be open to adjusting your plans or shifting your perspective when faced with unexpected obstacles. Flexibility and adaptability can help you navigate through challenging situations more effectively.

Remember, setbacks and challenges are part of the journey towards personal growth and success. Embrace them as opportunities to learn, grow, and become stronger. With a positive mindset, support from others, and a resilient attitude, you can overcome challenges and continue moving forward in life.

- Offer strategies to overcome obstacles and stay motivated.

Overcoming obstacles and staying motivated can be challenging, but with the right strategies, you can navigate through them. Here are some strategies to help you overcome obstacles and stay motivated:

1. Set clear goals: Clearly define your short-term and long-term goals. Having a clear vision of what you want to achieve will help you stay focused and motivated, even when faced with obstacles.

2. Break it down: Break your goals into smaller, more manageable tasks. This makes them less overwhelming and allows you to track your progress, which can boost motivation. Celebrate small victories along the way to stay motivated.

3. Create a plan: Develop a detailed plan of action to reach your goals. Outline the steps you need to take and the resources or support you might need. A well-structured plan can help you stay

organized and motivated, as it provides a roadmap for success.

4. Seek support: Surround yourself with a supportive network of friends, family, or mentors who can provide encouragement, advice, or assistance when needed. Sharing your challenges and progress with others can help you stay motivated and gain valuable insights.

5. Stay positive and practice self-compassion: Maintain a positive mindset and focus on your strengths and achievements. When facing obstacles, be kind to yourself and practice self-compassion. Treat setbacks as learning opportunities and remind yourself that you have the ability to overcome challenges.

6. Stay focused on the why: Remember why you started on this journey in the first place. Connect with your passion and purpose. When you have a strong sense of purpose, it can serve as a powerful motivator to keep going, even in the face of obstacles.

7. Embrace failure as part of the process: Understand that failure is a natural part of growth and success. Instead of being discouraged by setbacks, view them as learning experiences. Analyze what went wrong, make adjustments, and keep moving forward.

8. Take care of yourself: Prioritize self-care to maintain your physical and mental well-being. Get enough sleep, eat nutritious food, exercise regularly, and engage in activities that rejuvenate and energize you. When you take care of yourself, you have more resilience and motivation to face challenges.

9. Visualize success: Use the power of visualization to imagine yourself overcoming obstacles and achieving your goals. Visualize the positive outcomes and the feelings of success. This can help boost your motivation and keep you focused on the desired results.

10. Stay flexible and adaptable: Be open to adjusting your plans

or strategies when faced with unexpected obstacles. Flexibility and adaptability can help you find alternative solutions and keep moving forward.

Remember, staying motivated and overcoming obstacles is a journey. Be patient with yourself, stay persistent, and celebrate your progress along the way.

- Encourage the reader to persevere through tough times.

During tough times, it's important to remember that perseverance is key. Life can present us with numerous challenges and obstacles, but it's often in these moments that we have the opportunity to grow and discover our true strength. So, I want to encourage you to persevere through tough times with these thoughts in mind:

1. Remember your past successes: Reflect on the times when you faced difficult situations and came out stronger on the other side. Remind yourself of your resilience and the victories you have achieved before. This will give you the confidence to believe that you can overcome the current challenges as well.

2. Focus on the bigger picture: Keep your eyes on your long-term goals and aspirations. Remember why you started on this journey and what you hope to achieve. By keeping the bigger picture in mind, you can find the motivation and determination to push through the tough times.

3. Embrace the power of mindset: Your mindset plays a crucial role in how you approach and overcome challenges. Cultivate a positive mindset and believe in your ability to overcome obstacles. Replace self-doubt with self-belief and view challenges as opportunities for growth and learning.

4. Seek support from others: Don't hesitate to reach out for support when you need it. Surround yourself with a strong support system of friends, family, or mentors who can provide

guidance, encouragement, and a listening ear. Together, you can overcome even the toughest of times.

5. Break it down into smaller steps: Sometimes, facing a large obstacle can feel overwhelming. Break it down into smaller, more manageable steps. Focus on tackling one step at a time, celebrating each small victory along the way. This approach will help you maintain momentum and build confidence as you progress.

6. Practice self-care: Taking care of yourself is crucial during tough times. Prioritize self-care activities that help you relax, recharge, and reduce stress. This could include exercise, meditation, spending time in nature, pursuing hobbies, or simply taking time for yourself. By nurturing your well-being, you'll be better equipped to face challenges head-on.

7. Remind yourself of your purpose: Reconnect with your purpose and the reasons why you're persevering through tough times. Your purpose is the fuel that ignites your motivation and reminds you of the impact you can make. Stay focused on your purpose, and let it guide you through the difficult moments.

8. Celebrate small victories: Recognize and celebrate the small wins along the way. Acknowledge your progress, no matter how small it may seem. By doing so, you'll build confidence, maintain motivation, and create a positive mindset that propels you forward.

Remember, tough times don't last forever. By persevering and staying resilient, you'll emerge stronger and wiser on the other side. Believe in yourself, stay determined, and keep moving forward. You've got this!

Dear Readers,

Thank you so much for your purchase! I truly appreciate your support and hope that the book brings you valuable insights and inspiration.

Your feedback is incredibly important to me. If you have a few moments to spare, I kindly ask you to leave an honest review of the book. Your review will not only help me understand how I can improve, but it will also guide potential readers in making informed decisions.

I value your opinion and would love to hear about your experience with the book. Your feedback will assist me in creating more meaningful content and serving my readers better.

Once again, thank you for your purchase and for considering leaving a review. I'm grateful for your support and hope to continue providing you with valuable resources in the future.

Mark Livingston